Hot Math Topics

Problem Solving, Communication, and Reasoning

Addition and Subtraction

grade 2

Carole Greenes
Linda Schulman Dacey
Rika Spungin

Dale Seymour Publications®
White Plains, New York

DALE SEYMOUR PUBLICATIONS®

This book is published by Dale Seymour Publications®,
an imprint of Addison Wesley Longman, Inc.

Dale Seymour Publications
10 Bank Street
White Plains, New York 10602
Customer Service: 800-872-1100

Managing Editor: Catherine Anderson
Senior Editor: John Nelson
Project Editor: Mali Apple
Production/Manufacturing Director: Janet Yearian
Sr. Production/Manufacturing Coordinator: Fiona Santoianni
Design Director: Phyllis Aycock
Illustrations: Jared Lee
Text and Cover Design: Tracey Munz
Composition and Computer Graphics: Alan Noyes

Order number 21873
ISBN 0-7690-0015-0

This Book Is Printed
On Recycled Paper

contents

Introduction 1

Management Chart 6

Award Certificate 6

Problems and Tasks 7

Answers 58

Introduction

Why Was *Hot Math Topics* Developed?

The *Hot Math Topics* series was developed for several reasons:

- to offer children practice and maintenance of previously learned skills and concepts
- to enhance problem solving and mathematical reasoning abilities
- to build literacy skills
- to nurture collaborative learning behaviors

Practicing and maintaining concepts and skills

Although textbooks and core curriculum materials do treat the topics explored in this series, their treatment is often limited by the lesson format and the page size. As a consequence, there are often not enough opportunities for children to practice newly acquired concepts and skills related to the topics, or to connect the topics to other content areas. *Hot Math Topics* provides the necessary practice and mathematical connections.

Similarly, core instructional programs often do not do a very good job of helping children maintain their skills. Although textbooks do include reviews of previously learned material, they are often limited to sidebars or boxed-off areas on one or two pages in each chapter, with four or five exercises in each box. Each set of problems is intended only as a sampling of previously taught topics, rather than as a complete review. In the selection and placement of the review exercises, little or no attention

is given to levels of complexity of the problems. By contrast, *Hot Math Topics* targets specific topics and gives children more experience with concepts and skills related to them. The problems are sequenced by difficulty, allowing children to hone their skills. And, because they are not tied to specific lessons, the problems can be used at any time.

Enhancing problem solving and mathematical reasoning abilities

Hot Math Topics present children with situations in which they may use a variety of problem solving strategies, including

- designing and conducting experiments to generate or collect data
- guessing, checking, and revising guesses
- organizing data in lists or tables in order to identify patterns and relationships
- choosing appropriate computational algorithms and deciding on a sequence of computations
- using inverse operations in "work backward" solution paths

For their solutions, children are also required to bring to bear various methods of reasoning, including

- deductive reasoning
- inductive reasoning
- proportional reasoning

For example, to solve clue-type problems, children must reason deductively and make inferences about mathematical relationships in order to generate candidates for the solutions and to home in on those that meet all of the problem's conditions.

To identify and continue a pattern and then write a rule for finding the next term in that pattern, children must reason inductively.

To compute unit prices and make trades, children must reason proportionally.

To estimate or compare magnitudes of numbers, or to determine the type of number appropriate for a given situation, children must apply their number sense skills.

Building communication and literacy skills

Hot Math Topics offers children opportunities to write and talk about mathematical ideas. For many problems, children must describe their solution paths, justify their solutions, give their opinions, or write or tell stories.

Some problems have multiple solution methods. With these problems, children may have to compare their methods with those of their peers and talk about how their approaches are alike and different.

Other problems have multiple solutions, requiring children to confer to be sure they have found all possible answers.

Nurturing collaborative learning behaviors

Several of the problems can be solved by children working together. Some are designed specifically as partner problems. By working collaboratively, children can develop expertise in posing questions that call for clarification or verification, brainstorming solution strategies, and following another person's line of reasoning.

What Is in *Addition and Subtraction?*

This book contains 100 problems and tasks that focus on addition and subtraction. The mathematics content, the mathematical connections, the problem solving strategies, and the communication skills that are emphasized are described below.

Mathematics content

Addition and subtraction problems and tasks require children to

- add or subtract with up to three-digit numbers
- add with three or more addends
- add and subtract with money
- compare numbers and quantities
- estimate sums and differences
- use number sense to match numbers to given situations
- interpret the language of addition and subtraction word problems

Mathematical connections

In these problems and tasks, connections are made to these other topic areas:

- algebra
- geometry
- graphs
- measurement
- statistics
- number theory

Problem solving strategies

Addition and Subtraction problems and tasks offer children opportunities to use one or more of several problem solving strategies.

- **Formulate Questions:** When data are presented in displays or text form, children must pose one or more questions that can be answered using the given data.

- **Complete Stories:** When confronted with an incomplete story, children must supply the missing information and then check that the story makes sense.

- **Organize Information:** To ensure that several solution candidates for a problem are considered, children may have to organize information by drawing a picture, making a list, or completing a table.

- **Guess, Check, and Revise:** In some problems, children have to identify or generate candidates for the solution and then check whether those candidates match the conditions of the problem. If the conditions are not satisfied, other possible solutions must be generated and verified.

- **Identify and Continue Patterns:** To identify the next term or terms in a sequence, children have to recognize the relationship between successive terms and then generalize that relationship.

- **Use Logic:** Children have to reason deductively, from clues, to make inferences about the solution to a problem. They have to reason inductively to continue numeric patterns.

- **Work Backward:** In some problems, the output is given and children must determine the input by identifying mathematical relationships between the input and output and applying inverse operations.

Communication skills

Problems and tasks in *Addition and Subtraction* are designed to stimulate communication. As part of the solution process, children may have to

- describe their thinking steps
- describe patterns and rules
- find alternate solution methods and solution paths
- identify other possible answers
- formulate problems for classmates to solve
- compare solutions and methods with classmates
- make drawings to clarify mathematical relationships

These communication skills are enhanced when children interact with one another and with the teacher. By communicating both orally and in writing, children develop their understanding and use of the language of mathematics.

How Can *Hot Math Topics* Be Used?

The problems may be used as practice of newly learned concepts and skills, as maintenance of previously learned ideas, and as enrichment experiences for early finishers or more advanced students.

They may be used in class or assigned for homework. If used during class, they may be selected to complement lessons dealing with a specific topic or assigned every week as a means of keeping skills alive and well. Because the problems often require the application of various problem solving strategies and reasoning methods, they may also form the basis of whole-class lessons whose goals are to develop expertise with specific problem solving strategies or methods.

The problems may be used by children working in pairs or on their own. The problems are sequenced from least to most difficult. The selection of problems may be made by the teacher or the children based on their needs or interests. If the plan is for children to choose problems, you may wish to copy individual problems onto card stock and laminate them, and establish a problem card file.

To facilitate record keeping, a Management Chart is provided on page 6. The chart can be duplicated so that there is one for each child. As a problem is completed, the space corresponding to that problem's number may be shaded. An Award Certificate is included on page 6 as well.

How Can Children's Performance Be Assessed?

Addition and Subtraction problems and tasks provide you with opportunities to assess children's

- computation ability with addition and subtraction
- problem solving abilities
- mathematical reasoning methods
- communication skills

Observations

Keeping anecdotal records helps you to remember important information you gain as you observe children at work. To make observations more manageable, limit each observation to a group of from four to six children or to one of the areas noted above. You may find that using index cards facilitates the recording process.

Discussions

Many of the *Addition and Subtraction* problems and tasks allow for multiple answers or may be solved in a variety of ways. This built-in richness motivates children to discuss their work with one another. Small groups or class discussions are appropriate. As children share their approaches to the problems, you will gain additional insights into their content knowledge, mathematical reasoning, and communication abilities.

Scoring responses

You may wish to holistically score children's responses to the problems and tasks. The simple scoring rubric below uses three levels: high, medium, and low.

Portfolios

Having children store their responses to the problems in *Hot Math Topics* portfolios allows them to see improvement in their

High	Medium	Low
• Solution demonstrates that the child knows the concepts and skills.	• Solution demonstrates that the child has some knowledge of the concepts and skills.	• Solution shows that the child has little or no grasp of the concepts and skills.
• Solution is complete and thorough.	• Solution is complete.	• Solution is incomplete or contains major errors.
• The child communicates effectively.	• The child communicates somewhat clearly.	• The child does not communicate effectively.

work over time. You may want to have them choose examples of their best responses for inclusion in their permanent portfolios, accompanied by explanations as to why each was chosen.

Children and the assessment process

Involving children in the assessment process is central to the development of their abilities to reflect on their own work, to understand the assessment standards to which they are held accountable, and to take ownership for their own learning. Young children may find the reflective process difficult, but with your coaching, they can develop such skills.

Discussion may be needed to help children better understand your standards for performance. Ask children such questions as, "What does it mean to communicate *clearly*?" "What is a *complete* response?" Some children may want to use the high-medium-low rubric to score their responses. Others may prefer to use a simple visual evaluation, such as these characters:

Participation in peer-assessment tasks will also help children to better understand the performance standards. In pairs or small groups, children can review each other's responses and offer feedback. Opportunities to revise work may then be given.

What Additional Materials Are Needed?

Drawing tools (colored pencils, crayons, and rulers), cubes, a paper bag, and file cards are required for some of the problems in *Addition and Subtraction*. Other manipulative materials may be helpful, including base ten blocks, centimeter graph paper, and Cuisenaire rods.

Management Chart

Name _____

When a problem or task is completed, shade the box with that number.

1	2	3	4	5	6	7	8	9	10
11	12	13	14	15	16	17	18	19	20
21	22	23	24	25	26	27	28	29	30
31	32	33	34	35	36	37	38	39	40
41	42	43	44	45	46	47	48	49	50
51	52	53	54	55	56	57	58	59	60
61	62	63	64	65	66	67	68	69	70
71	72	73	74	75	76	77	78	79	80
81	82	83	84	85	86	87	88	89	90
91	92	93	94	95	96	97	98	99	100

Award Certificate

Hot Math Topics
SUPER SOLVER

this certifies that

_____

has been awarded the Hot Math Topics Super Solver Certificate for

Excellence in Problem Solving

_____   _____
date   signature

Problems
and Tasks

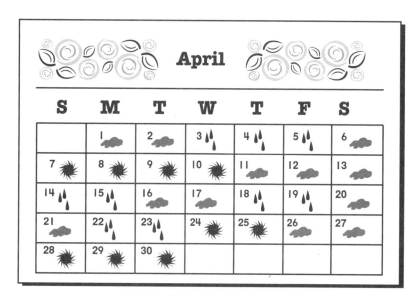

April

S	M	T	W	T	F	S
	1	2	3	4	5	6
7	8	9	10	11	12	13
14	15	16	17	18	19	20
21	22	23	24	25	26	27
28	29	30				

☀ sunny
☁ cloudy
☂ rainy

How many more days were ☁ or ☂ than ☀ ?

- -

Pick 2 of these numbers.
Find the sum.

5 6 7 8 10

How many different sums can you make?
Show the sums.

3

What number am I?

- I am greater than 6 + 7.

- I am less than 9 + 9.

- You say me when you count by twos.

- I am not 8 + 8.

- -

4

Target Sum 18

Play this game several times with a friend.

- Player 1 writes one of the numbers 1, 2, or 3.

- Player 2 adds 1, 2, or 3 to the number.

- Take turns adding 1, 2, or 3 to the sum.

- The winner is the player who gets 18.

Suppose the sum is 14 and it is your turn.

Can you win? Explain.

Marla put 2 chips in each cup.

How many chips are not in cups?

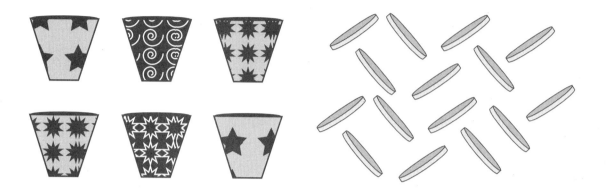

Tell how you know.

- -

Start with 4. End with 4.

Follow the arrows.

Write the last clue on the line.

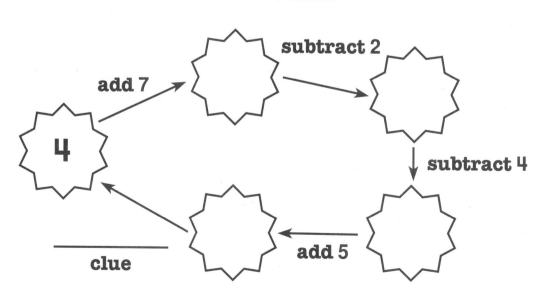

add 7

subtract 2

subtract 4

add 5

_____
clue

Row 1	✿ ✿ ✿ ✿
Row 2	✿ ✿ ✿ ✿ ✿ ✿
Row 3	✿ ✿ ✿ ✿ ✿ ✿ ✿ ✿
Row 4	✿ ✿ ✿ ✿
Row 5	✿ ✿ ✿
Row 6	

How many ✿ are in row 6?

Tell how you know.

- -

Circle 2 numbers.

Their sum is 12.

Their difference is 2.

7	8
4	5

Circle 2 numbers.

Their sum is 17.

Their difference is 1.

9	8
10	7

What number is on box 6?

How do you know?

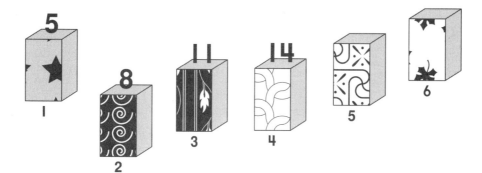

Talk with a friend about your ideas.

Start with 20. Pick a countdown number.

Count down by your number.

Does the countdown end on 0?

If not, try another countdown number.

Which countdown numbers end on 0?

Let's see.
Start with 20.
Count down by fives:
20, 15, 10, 5, 0.
The countdown ends on 0.

©Addison Wesley Longman, Inc./Published by Dale Seymour Publications®

©Addison Wesley Longman, Inc./Published by Dale Seymour Publications®

Favorite Numbers

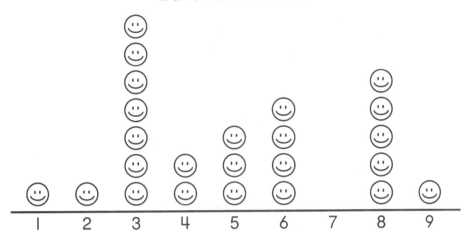

11

Each 😊 stands for one child.

How many children did not pick 6 or 3 as their favorite number?

Tell how you know.

Write in numbers so that the story makes sense.

12

José loves fruit.

In one week, he ate _____ bananas and _____ apples.

He ate _____ more bananas than apples.

Altogether he ate _____ pieces of fruit.

Hani used 2 red blocks and 4 blue blocks to build a tower.

How many blocks are left that are not blue?

Tell how you know.

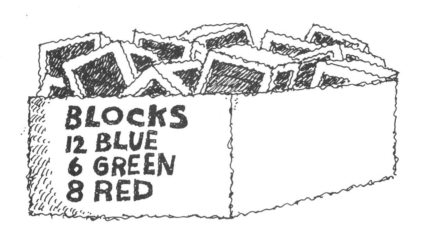

BLOCKS
12 BLUE
6 GREEN
8 RED

Use the facts.

Write a question for each answer on the Answer Sign.

Facts

- Jill has 5 raisins.
- Mike has 12 raisins.
- Lucia has 11 raisins.

ANSWER SIGN
6
1
17 28

How many more children chose apples or bananas than pears?

Favorite Fruit

Number of children

15
12
9
6
3

apples · bananas · pears

Type of fruit

Ask another question about the graph.

Answer your question.

Toss 3 rings.

If all 3 rings land on pegs, can you score 21?

If yes, tell how.

Key
circle = 4 points
rectangle = 3 points

|| points

Draw 2 different ways to get 15 points.

15 points

15 points

Find the ages of the sisters.

In 6 years I will be 13.
I am _____ years old.

I am the baby in the family.
I am 2 years younger than Beth.
I am _____ years old.

I am 11 years older
than Beth.
I am _____ years old.

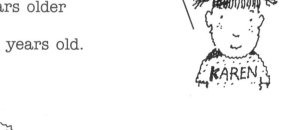

When you count by fives,
you say my age.
I am in kindergarten.
I am _____ years old.

19

How much more do 2 bats cost than
2 balls?

Give 2 ways to solve the problem.

- -

20

Fill in the missing prices above.

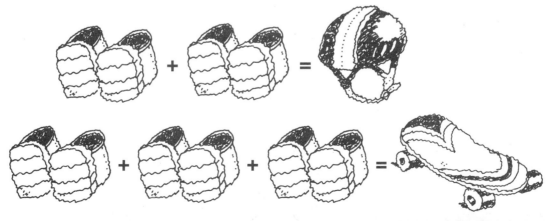

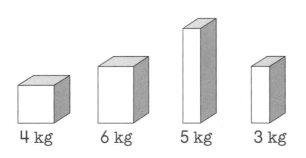

4 kg   6 kg   5 kg   3 kg

You have lots of blocks like these.

How many different ways can you put 12 kg on the scale?

Make a list.

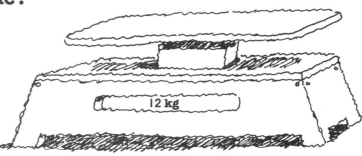

12 kg

- -

Carnival Rides

Ride	Tickets
Ferris wheel	5
Merry-go-round	3
Roller coaster	6
Go carts	8

You have 40 tickets.

You have time for 7 rides.

Which rides will you choose?

How many tickets will you have left?

Conduct an experiment.

23

- Make number cards for 1, 3, 5, 7, 9, and 11.
- Put them in a paper bag.
- Shake the bag.
- Pull out 2 number cards. Record the sum.
- Put the cards back in the bag.

Do this 20 times.

Tell about the results of your experiment.

24

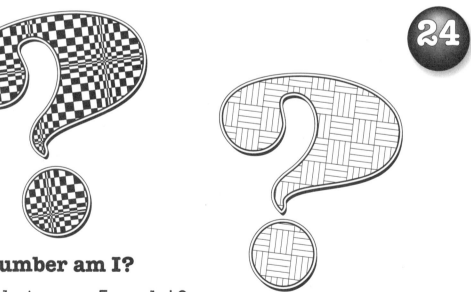

What number am I?

- I am between 5 and 10.
- Double me and subtract 1, and you get 15.

Now write your own clues for the number 12.

How many pounds?

 = _____ pounds

 = _____ pounds

These stickers are for sale.

| 3¢ | 2¢ | 7¢ |

Make a sticker design that costs 20¢.

Now make a different design that costs 20¢.

Give each letter in your name 2 points.

Find the total number of points for vowels.

Find the total number of points for consonants.

Which total is greater? How much greater?

Compare your totals with friends' totals.

Who is in grade 2?

- Todd is 3 years older than Kiran.
- Kiran is 10 years younger than Chad.
- Chad is 14 years old.

29

Put the same number in each .

 +  **< 10**

What numbers could be in the  ?

- -

30

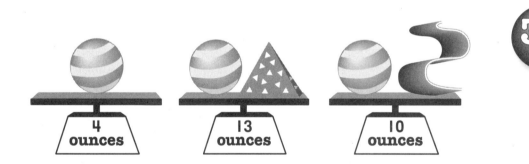

How many ounces?

Fill in the blanks with numbers.

The numbers must make sense.

_____ + _____ + _____ = 8

_____ + _____ − _____ = 8

_____ − _____ − _____ = 8

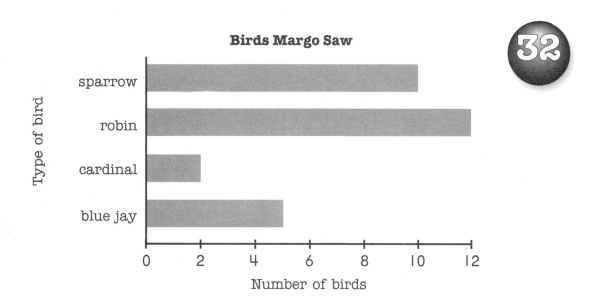

Birds Margo Saw

How many more sparrows than cardinals did Margo see?

Tell two ways to find out.

This is a +4 addition pattern.

Add 4 to each number.

0, 4, 8, ____, ____, ____, ____,

____, ____, ____, ____, ____,

Make up a different addition pattern.

Fill in the blanks.

0, ____, ____, ____, ____, ____,

____, ____, ____, ____, ____, ____

$30

$12

soccer ball = $ _____

sports mug = $ _____

Two years ago Maria was 7 years old.

How old will she be next year?

Tell how you know.

- -

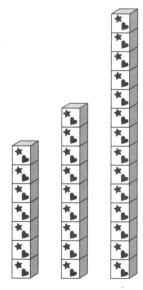

Make 3 block towers like these.

Move blocks to make all 3 towers the same height.

How many blocks are in each tower now?

Play Take-Away with a friend.

- Start with 12.
- Take turns.
- Subtract 1 or 2.
- The player whose answer is 0 wins.

Play 5 times.

Suppose it is your turn.
The answer your friend gave is 4.
What will you subtract, 1 or 2?
Tell why.

Diedre has 6 cousins.

Lucy has 8 more cousins than Diedre.

Nathan has 3 fewer cousins than Lucy.

How many cousins does Nathan have?

Name _____

Write 9 <u>different</u> problems with an answer of 9.

Use <u>addition</u> and <u>subtraction</u> only.

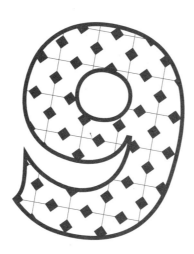

- -

MUFFINS 30¢   CARROT CAKE 1 SLICE 40¢   FRUIT BARS 20¢

You have 60¢.

Find 3 ways to spend all your money at the bakery.

You toss 3 hoops.

Each hoop scores.

What different total scores could you get?

Make a list.

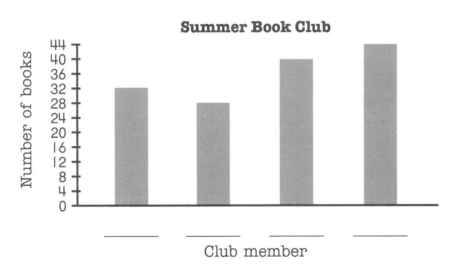

Summer Book Club

The graph shows how many books each club member read.

Write the children's names on the lines.

- Hong read 8 more books than Gina.

- Gina read 4 more books than Tom.

- Gina read 12 books fewer than Anya.

Draw apples on the plates.

You have 10 apples.

Draw 2 more apples on B than on A.

Draw 3 more apples on C than on B.

Plate A   Plate B   Plate C

How many apples are on A?

Talk with a friend about how you know.

- -

Write numbers to finish the pattern.

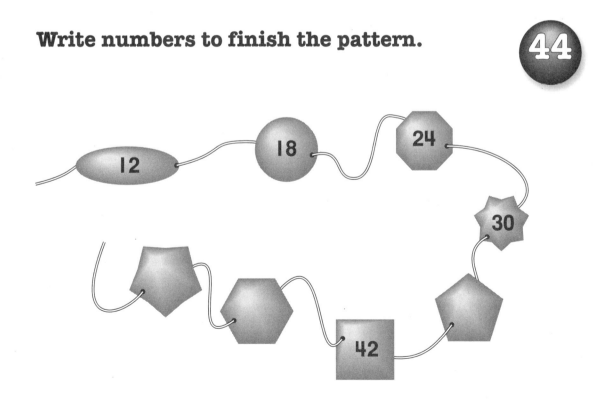

Put numbers in the shapes.

Put the same number in the same shapes.

⬡ + ⬡ = 14

⬡ + ☆ = 10

⬡ = _____   ☆ = _____

- -

How long is this train?

45

46

Use lengths like these.

| 2 cm | 3 cm | 4 cm |

Make a train 13 centimeters long.

Compare your train with a friend's train.

Draw lines from each price tag to an item.

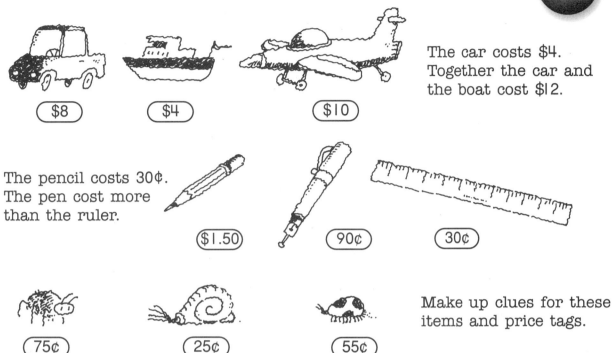

The car costs $4.
Together the car and
the boat cost $12.

$8 $4 $10

The pencil costs 30¢.
The pen cost more
than the ruler.

$1.50   90¢   30¢

Make up clues for these
items and price tags.

75¢   25¢   55¢

- -

Draw a bead chain with a length of 18 cm.
Use these beads.

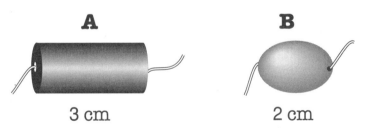

A

3 cm

B

2 cm

Draw 3 more bead chains with a length of 18 cm.

Make sure all your bead chains are different.

Tell how many A beads and how many B beads you use in each chain.

Think of a number greater than 7.

Write it here.

Add 4.

Subtract 10.

Subtract 2.

Add 8.

What did you get?

Start with another number. What do you get?

Why do you think that always happens?

Move one number from one circle to another circle.

After the move, the sum of the numbers in each circle must be 36.

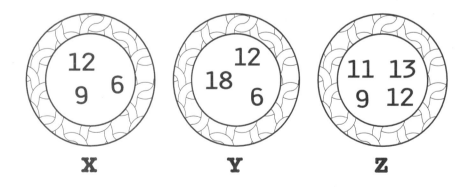

X   Y   Z

Circle X: 12 9 6

Circle Y: 12 18 6

Circle Z: 11 13 9 12

Which number did you move?

Where did you move it?

51

Pick a number from the balloons.

Write an addition story problem that has this number as the answer.

Do the same for the other numbers.

- -

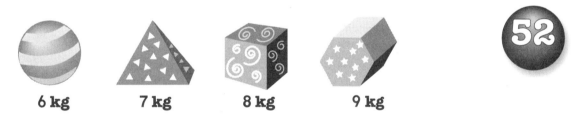

6 kg   7 kg   8 kg   9 kg

52

Draw shapes on the scale to make it balance.

Use all 4 shapes.

Write the numbers on the shapes.

This is a magic T.

The sum of the numbers across equals
the sum of the numbers down.

Magic Sum = 15

	9	
3	5	7
	1	

Use the numbers shown
to make a different
magic T.

Magic Sum = 18

6

10

2

4

8

I am thinking of 2 numbers.

When I add the numbers, I get 20.

When I subtract one from the other, I get 2.

What are my numbers?

This glass holds 8 ounces of water.

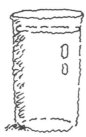

About how many ounces of water are in these glasses altogether?

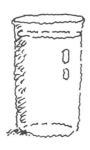   

- -

I bought 3 different books.

I gave the clerk $20.

I got $4 in change.

Which books did I buy?

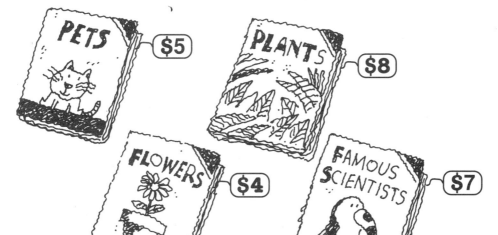

 = 10

☆ − ❀ = 6

What number is ☆ ?   What number is ❀ ?

Tell how you decided.

- -

worms

stones

spiders

lizards

29

Pick 2 of the numbers.
Pick 2 of the words.
Write an addition story problem.

7

Pick 2 different numbers.
Pick 2 different words.
Write a subtraction story problem.

9

Give the problems to a friend to solve.

15

Check the answers.

This is a magic triangle.

The sum of the 3 numbers on each side is 9.

Use the numbers shown to make a new magic triangle.

Magic Sum = 9   (59)

Magic Sum = 12

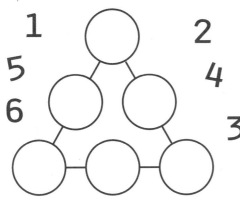

1   2

5   4

6   3

- -

Louis, Pam, and Ali compare their heights.   (60)

Louis is 9 inches taller than Pam.

Pam is 5 inches shorter than Ali.

Ali is 50 inches tall.

How tall is Pam?

How tall is Louis?

Complete the grid.

Add 5 going across.

Add 6 going up.

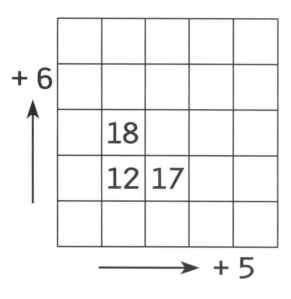

+ 6

18

12 17

⟶ + 5

- -

Use the facts.

Write a question for each answer on the Answer Sign.

Facts

- Lee bought 16 star stickers and 10 rainbow stickers.

- Niki bought 9 star stickers and 15 rainbow stickers.

Answer Sign

26   50   7
         5

Pick a number from the balloons.

Write a subtraction story problem that has this number as the answer.

Do the same for the other numbers.

- -

Work with a friend.

Each of you fill in the blanks.

The sentences must be true.

12 is ____
more than ____ .

12 is ____
less than ____ .

Compare your sentences with your friend's sentences.

65

Ms. Avila bought 2 boxes of birthday cards
and 1 box of thank-you cards.

Mr. Williams bought 2 boxes of thank-you
cards.

How many more cards did Ms. Avila buy
than Mr. Williams?

Tell 2 ways to decide.

Gena had some carrot sticks.

She ate 3 of the carrot sticks.

She gave 4 carrot sticks to Malia.

She has 2 carrot sticks left.

How many carrot sticks did Gena
have at the start?

66

CAB is 6 points: 3 + 1 + 2 = 6.

What other words can you write with the letters on the sign?

How many points is each word?

Which word is worth the most points?

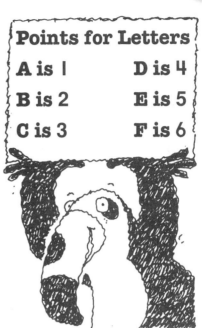

Points for Letters	
A is 1	D is 4
B is 2	E is 5
C is 3	F is 6

---

95 56 12 36 23

Use the numbers given.

Estimate to help you decide how to fill in the blanks.

_____ + _____ = 48

_____ + _____ = 92

_____ − _____ = 72

_____ − _____ = 33

Tell the patterns that you see.

Use the patterns to help you fill in the blanks.

1 + 2 + 3 = 6
2 + 3 + 4 = 9
3 + 4 + 5 = 12
4 + _____ + _____ = _____
_____ + _____ + _____ = _____

_____ + _____ + _____ = 30

- -

Use these numbers.

9   6   8   3

**Use each number once.
Make the greatest sum.**

**Use each number once.
Make the greatest difference.**

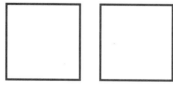

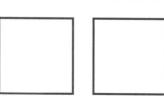

Fill in the blanks with numbers.

The story must make sense.

There were _____ ears of corn in the garden.

Ben picked _____ ears.

_____ ears were left in the garden.

Ben's father cooked the corn.

Ben's family ate _____ of these ears of corn for dinner.

_____ ears of corn were left after dinner.

Use the numbers shown.

Use each number only once.

Write the numbers in the circles.

Each row of 3 numbers must add to 16.

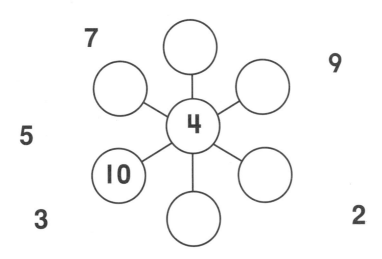

7

9

5

3

2

73

Suppose you start at 100 and keep subtracting 7 until you get close to 0.

Will you land on any even numbers?

If yes, which numbers?

- -

Estimate sums to help you decide where to place the numbers.

74

Use each number once.

_____ + _____ is 100.

_____ + _____ is less than 100.

_____ + _____ is more than 100.

39   48   90   27   52   123

There are coins in the banks.

The numbers tell how many coins are in 2 banks.

piggy + dolphin	dolphin + duck	duck + piggy
5 coins	6 coins	7 coins

How many coins are in each bank?

piggy
bank: _____

dolphin
bank: _____

duck
bank: _____

- -

Each apple weighs about 5 ounces.

About how many ounces does each banana weigh?

Tell the steps you used to solve the problem.

Use each number only once.

Complete the number sentences.

_____ + _____ = 15

_____ + _____ = 15

_____ + _____ + _____ + _____ + _____ = 15

- -

Complete the grid.

Subtract 4 going across.

Subtract 9 going up.

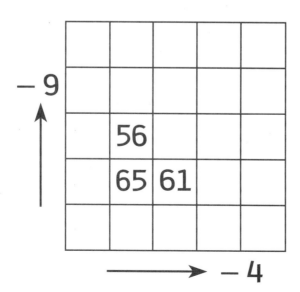

$$0 \quad 1 \quad 2 \quad 3$$
$$4 \quad 5 \quad 6 \quad 7 \quad 8$$
$$9 \quad 10 \quad 11 \quad 12$$

You have lots of 2s and 3s.

You can add or subtract.

Circle the numbers you can make.

Show how you made them.

Examples: $3 + 3 + 2 = 8$

$3 + 3 + 3 + 3 - 2 - 2 = 8$

- -

Janice drove from Gravel to Boulder and back. She took the shortest route.

Andre drove from Gravel to Rocktown to Cliff City and back to Gravel.

How many more kilometers did Janice drive than Andre?

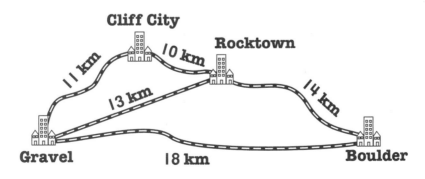

Write your own "driving question" about the map.

Give your question to a friend.

Perimeter is the distance around something.

81

Find the perimeter of the rectangle.

3 cm

10 cm

Draw 2 other rectangles with the same perimeter as this one.

- -

The numbers in circles are the sums of the rows and the columns.

82

A	A	2	12
0	B	9	11
C	3	C	15
11	10	17	

A = _____   B = _____   C = _____

Who am I?

When you add me to 25, you get 47.

When you subtract me from 55, you get _____.

I am _____.

Who am I?

When you subtract me from 30, you get 12.

When you add me to 9, you get _____.

I am _____.

Write your own "Who am I?" problem.

Give it to a friend to solve.

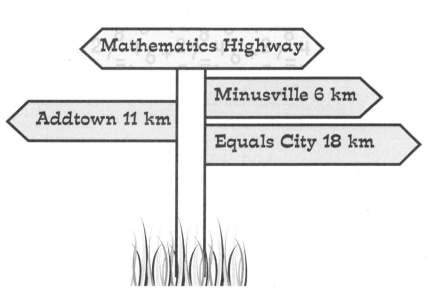

You are on Mathematics Highway.

How much farther is it from Addtown to Equals City than it is from Addtown to Minusville?

Tell how you know.

Add.

Decide where each sum is on the number line.

Write the sum under the dot.

$17 + 2$ $10 + 3$

0 |----|--|--|--|--|--|•|--|•|--|--|--|•|--|•|--|--|•|--|--| 40

___   ___   ___ ___   ___

$23 + 7$ $22 + 5$ $6 + 30$

- -

Play this game with a friend. Take turns.

Pick 2 numbers from the Number Box.

Subtract the lesser number from the greater number.

Find the difference on the Game Board. Color it.

Try to get 3 in a row: → ↓ ↘ or ↗.

Number Box

99	
	88
76	
	32
93	
	20

Game Board

79	17	67	44
12	5	56	68
61	6	12	56
23	70	11	73

What is the number?

- It is less than 42 + 36.
- It is greater than 17 + 22.
- It is not equal to 28 + 34.

Write clues to find another number on the sign.

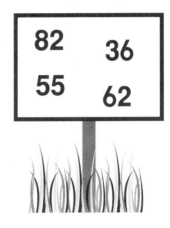

82	36
55	62

Marcia's class took a survey to find out what cookies people like.

Use the clues.

Write the names of the cookies on the lines.

Clues

- Ginger snaps got the fewest votes.
- Chocolate chip got the most votes.
- 29 more people voted for chocolate chip than for peanut butter.
- More people voted for oatmeal than for butterscotch.

Cookie Survey

Cookie	Votes
_____	12
_____	44
_____	6
_____	15
_____	32

89

Put the same number in each box.

$$\begin{array}{r} 16 \\ \square \\ \square \\ + \ \square \\ \hline 61 \end{array}$$

Tell how you found the number.

90

Find the missing digits.

$$\begin{array}{rrr} 4 & \bigcirc & 6 \\ - \ \bigcirc & 5 & 2 \\ \hline & 3 & \bigcirc \end{array}$$

Make up a missing-digits problem.

Give it to a friend to solve.

©Addison Wesley Longman, Inc./Published by Dale Seymour Publications®

Look for patterns.

Fill in the blanks.

Tell 3 things about the patterns you see.

$$32 - 15 = 17$$
$$28 - 13 = 15$$
$$24 - 11 = 13$$
$$20 - \ 9 = \underline{\hspace{1.5cm}}$$
$$16 - \underline{\hspace{0.8cm}} = \underline{\hspace{1.5cm}}$$
$$\underline{\hspace{0.8cm}} - \underline{\hspace{0.8cm}} = \underline{\hspace{1.5cm}}$$
$$\underline{\hspace{0.8cm}} - \underline{\hspace{0.8cm}} = \underline{\hspace{1.5cm}}$$

Janny added 107 + 106 this way:

- **Step 1:** 6 + 7 = 13
- **Step 2:** 100 + 100 = 200
- **Step 3:** 200 + 13 = 213

Use Janny's method.

Write the steps for 208 + 209.

- **Step 1:**
- **Step 2:**
- **Step 3:**

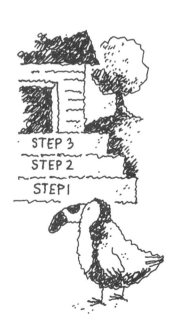

4   7   128   144

Use the numbers shown.

Write them on the lines.

The story must make sense.

Brad got _____ books and _____ videos for his birthday.

He got 3 more books than videos.

The book about rocks had more than 100 pages. It had _____ pages.

The rock book had 16 fewer pages than the book about inventors.

The inventors book had _____ pages.

Kai has 100 stamps.

- 32 stamps are from France.
- 16 stamps are from India.
- 13 stamps are from Japan.
- The rest of the stamps are from Egypt.

How many more of Kai's stamps are from Egypt than from France?

Play this game with a friend. Take turns.

Pick 1 number from **A** and 1 from **B**. Add.

Find the sum on the Game Board. Color it.

Try to get 4 in a row: →↓ ↘ or ↗.

95

Game Board

137	158	365	753
575	336	226	247
887	554	693	748
425	769	276	947

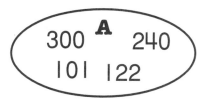

A
300   240
101   122

B
36   453
125   647

Suppose you know that

$$173 + 173 = 346$$

96

What shortcut can you use to solve

$$175 + 175 = ?$$

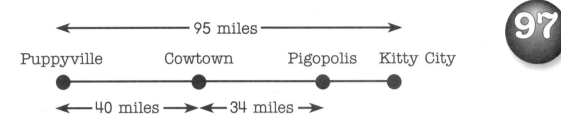

95 miles

Puppyville   Cowtown   Pigopolis   Kitty City

40 miles   34 miles

Use the map.

Fill in the chart to show the distances in miles.

From	To	Miles
Puppyville	Pigopolis	
Cowtown	Kitty City	
Pigopolis	Kitty City	

Write a number in each empty square of the puzzle.

Then write a clue for each "across" and "down" number.

Each clue must use + or −.

Clues

Across

1. 124 + 24

3.

5.

7.

Down

2.

4.

6.

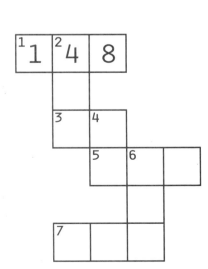

©Addison Wesley Longman, Inc./Published by Dale Seymour Publications®

©Addison Wesley Longman, Inc./Published by Dale Seymour Publications®

Start with a number.   85
Reverse the digits. Add.   + 58
                                            ———
                                            143
Reverse the digits. Add.   + 341
484 is a *palindrome*.   ———
                                            484
It reads the same forward and backward.

Try 39.

Reverse the digits. Add.

Keep reversing and adding until you get a palindrome.

Try 68 and 74. What palindromes do you get?

I bought a dog for $40.

I sold the dog for $50.

I bought the dog back for $60.

Juan said the dog cost me $100.

Lelia said the dog cost me $60.

Randy said the dog cost me $50.

Who is right?

Why?

Answers

1. 12 days

2. There are 8 different sums:
   $5 + 6 = 11, 5 + 7 = 12, 5 + 8 = 13$ or
   $6 + 7 = 13, 6 + 8 = 14, 5 + 10 = 15$ or
   $7 + 8 = 15, 6 + 10 = 16, 7 + 10 = 17$,
   and $8 + 10 = 18$.

3. 14

4. No; you can add 1, 2, or 3 to get 15, 16, or 17, and your friend will win by adding 3, 2, or 1, respectively, to get 18.

5. 3 chips; 2 chips in each of 6 cups is 12 chips in cups; $15 - 12 = 3$ chips not in cups.

6. 4, 11, 9, 5, 10, 4; subtract 6

7. 14; The number of ❀ increases by 2 for each row.

8. 7 and 5; 9 and 8

9. 20; Each box's number is 3 more than that of the preceding box.

10. 1, 2, 4, 5, 10, 20

11. 13 children; Count the ☺ above all numbers except 3 and 6.

12. Answers will vary. The number of bananas must be greater than the number of apples.

13. 12 blocks; Possible explanation: Subtract 2 from 8 red; add the remaining 6 red to 6 green.

14. Possible answer: How many more raisins does Lucia have than Jill? (6) How many raisins do Jill and Mike have in all? (17) How many more raisins does Mike have than Lucia? (1) How many raisins do Jill, Mike, and Lucia have in all? (28)

15. 6 children; Questions will vary.

16. yes; 2 rings on 6 and 1 ring on 9; or 1 ring each on 5, 7, and 9; or 3 rings on 7

17. 5 rectangles; 3 circles and 1 rectangle

18. Tanya, 7; Alex, 16; Beth, 5; Karen, 3

19. One bat costs $2 more than 1 ball, so 2 bats cost $2 × $2 = $4 more than 2 balls. Or, 2 bats cost $14, and 2 balls cost $10; $14 - $10 = $4.

20. skateboard, $27; knee pads, $9

21. 5 ways: two 6 kg; one 6 kg and two 3 kg; one 5 kg, one 4 kg, and one 3 kg; three 4 kg; four 3 kg

22. Answers will vary.

23. Results will vary, but all sums will be even.

24. 8; Clues will vary.

25. 7 pounds; 11 pounds

26. Designs might involve the following combinations:

◪	◆	✦
6	1	
4	4	
3	2	1
2	7	
2		2
1	5	1
	3	2
	10	

27. Answers will vary.

28. Todd, who is 7, is in grade 2.

29. any number less than 5

30. 19 ounces

31. Answers will vary.

32. 8; Possible explanation: Count up from cardinal to sparrow: 2, 4, 6, 8. Or, subtract the number of cardinals from the number of sparrows: $10 - 2 = 8$.

33. 12, 16, 20, 24, 28, 32, 36, 40, 44; Patterns will vary.

34. soccer ball, $24; sports mug, $6

35. 10 years old; This year she is $7 + 2 = 9$, so next year she will be 10.

36. 10 blocks

37. 1; If you subtract 2, leaving 2, your friend will win.

38. 11 cousins

39. Answers will vary.

40. Buy 2 muffins, 3 fruit bars, or 1 slice of carrot cake and 1 fruit bar.

41. 6, 9, 10, 12, 13, 14, 15, 16, 17, and 18 points

42. from left to right: Gina, Tom, Hong, Anya

43. A—1 apple, B—3 apples, C—6 apples; 1 apple; Explanations will vary.

44. 36, 48, 54

45. 7, 3

46. 11 cm; Trains will vary.

47. car, $4; boat, $8; plane, $10; pen, $1.50; pencil, 30¢; ruler, 90¢; Clues will vary.

48. 6 A and 0 B, 4 A and 3 B, 2 A and 6 B, 0 A and 9 B

49. The answer equals the starting number. Adding 4 and 8 is the same as adding 12, and subtracting 10 and 2 is the same as subtracting 12. This is like adding 0, which does not change the value of the starting number.

50. Move 9 from Z to X.

51. Story problems will vary.

52.

53. Possible answer:

	10	
8	6	4
	2	

54. 11 and 9

55. 28 ounces

56. *Pets, Flowers,* and *Famous Scientists*

57. 8, 2; Explanations will vary.

58. Story problems will vary.

59. Possible answer:

60. 45 inches; 54 inches

61.

25	30	35	40	45
19	24	29	34	39
13	18	23	28	33
7	12	17	22	27
1	6	11	16	21

62. Possible answer: How many stickers did Lee buy? (26) How many more star stickers does Lee have than Niki? (7) How many more rainbow stickers does Niki have than Lee? (5) How many stickers did Lee and Niki buy in all? (50)

63. Story problems will vary.

64. Answers will vary.

65. 4 cards; Possible explanation: Add to find the total number of cards Ms. Avila bought ($8 + 8 + 12 = 28$) and the total Mr. Williams bought ($12 + 12 = 24$), then subtract to find the difference ($28 - 24 = 4$). Or, since each bought 1 box of thank-you cards, eliminate it from each total: Ms. Avila bought 16 ($8 + 8$) and Mr. Williams bought 12, and $16 - 12 = 4$.

66. 9 carrot sticks

67. Some possible words: deeded (27); beaded (21); feed (20); faced (19); deed, beef (18); cafe, face (15); dead (14); bead, bee (12); bed, fad (11); ace (9)

68. 36 + 12 = 48   95 − 23 = 72
    56 + 36 = 92   56 − 23 = 33

69. Possible patterns: Each column of addends increases by 1. Numbers added in an equation are consecutive. Sums are multiples of 3. Sums are divisible by the second addend.
    4 + 5 + 6 = 15
    5 + 6 + 7 = 18
    9 + 10 + 11 = 30

70. 96 + 83 = 179 or 93 + 86 = 179; 98 − 36 = 62

71. Answers will vary.

72. Possible answer:

73. yes; 86, 72, 58, 44, 30, 16, 2

74. 52 + 48 = 100, 39 + 27 < 100, 123 + 90 > 100

75. piggy bank, 3 coins; dolphin bank, 2 coins; duck bank, 4 coins

76. 8 ounces; Possible explanation: 2 apples weigh 10 ounces, so 26 − 10 = 16 ounces for the 2 bananas, so each banana weighs 8 ounces (8 + 8 = 16).

77. 9 + 6 = 15, 7 + 8 = 15, 1 + 2 + 3 + 4 + 5 = 15

78.
42	38	34	30	26
51	47	43	39	35
60	56	52	48	44
69	65	61	57	53
78	74	70	66	62

79. You can make all the numbers. Explanations will vary.

80. 2 km; Questions will vary.

81. 26 cm; Possible rectangles: 1 by 12, 2 by 11, 4 by 9, 5 by 8, 6 by 7

82. A = 5, B = 2, C = 6

83. 33, 22; 27, 18; Problems will vary.

84. 12 km; Addtown to Equals City is 11 + 18 = 29 km. Addtown to Minusville is 11 + 6 = 17 km. Equals City is 29 − 17 = 12 km farther.

85. 13, 19, 27, 30, 36

87. 55; Clues will vary.

88. from the top: butterscotch, chocolate chip, ginger snaps, peanut butter, oatmeal

89. 15; Explanations will vary.

90. 486 − 452 = 34; Problems will vary.

91. 20 − 9 = 11
    16 − 7 = 9
    12 − 5 = 7
    8 − 3 = 5
    Possible patterns: Numbers in the first column are multiples of 4, each 4 less than the previous. Numbers in the second column are all odd, each 2 less than the previous. Numbers in the third column are all odd, each 2 less than the previous. Differences are all 2 greater than the numbers in the second column.

92. Step 1: 8 + 9 = 17
    Step 2: 200 + 200 = 400
    Step 3: 400 + 17 = 417

93. 7, 4, 128, 144

94. 7 stamps

96. Since 175 is 2 more than 173, 175 + 175 will be 4 more than 346, or 350.

97. from the top: 74, 55, 21

98. Puzzles and clues will vary.

99. for 39, 363; for 68, 1111; for 74, 121

100. Randy; I spent $100 and made $50, and $100 − $50 = $50.